Why Men A

Amy Charter

SUMMERSDALE

Summersdale Publishers Ltd
46 West Street
Chichester
West Sussex
PO19 1RP
United Kingdom

www.summersdale.com

ISBN 1 84024 127 6

Printed and bound in Great Britain

Cartoons by Kate Taylor

'Women who seek to be equal
with men lack ambition.'

Timothy Leary

Contents

Introduction

Why men are crap: a large tome would barely scratch the surface of such an extensive topic. But, for your convenience, here is a handy and concise pocket book with just the right amount of ammunition to fire at the nearest male – and get him where it hurts.

Whether you are a woman and want to pin-point exactly what it is that gets your goat about men, or whether you are a man who would like to learn how to improve himself (unlikely), you will enjoy these tongue-in-cheek nuggets of wisdom. Oh, and a last word to any man reading this – don't go into a sulk, will you?

Why Men are Crap . . .

Why *Men* Are Crap!

- Menstruation
- Mental Illness
- Menopause
- Meningitis

– Discomfort and illness always start with men.

Why *Men* Are Crap!

Women like cats.

Men say they like cats, but when women aren't looking, men kick cats.

Why *Men* Are Crap!

Ponytails on men can indeed look thick and lustrous – but on ponies they cover the whole arsehole.

Why *Men* Are Crap!

Men have selective hearing. There are certain keywords (football, sex, food, beer etc.) that he will hear, but on the whole it is futile trying to get a man to absorb anything you say. He may pretend he has been listening, but by the end of the day when he asks you about something that you have already told him, YOU WILL KNOW.

Why *Men* Are Crap!

Toilets, anniversaries, and erogenous zones all have one thing in common. Men always miss them.

Why *Men* Are Crap!

BEWARE: When you enter into a relationship with a man, not far behind him will be his possessive, son-worshipping, death-defying mother. Do not come between her and her golden boy if you value your life.

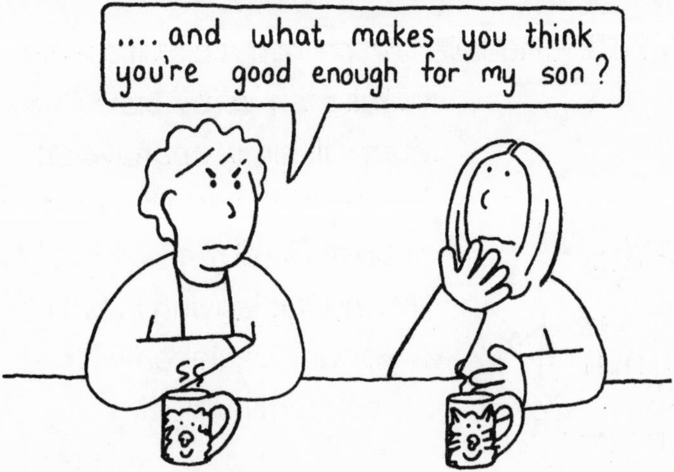
....and what makes you think you're good enough for my son?

Why *Men* Are Crap!

BEWARE: Men are too chicken to make a clean break from a relationship. A man will simply behave so badly that a woman will finish it first. Said man will disappear, leaving in his wake a woman furnished with an all-consuming guilt.

Why *Men* Are Crap!

Single women complain that all the good men are married, while married women complain about their lousy husbands. This confirms that there is no such thing as a good man.

Why *Men* Are Crap!

Never send a man out to buy a present. He is liable to buy something either completely

inappropriate (for example, a skipping rope for your disabled grandmother), or something completely cheesy (for example, a pink china kitten for The Woman in His Life).

Why *Men* Are Crap!

Men in drag: now who on earth can understand why anyone, given a comfortable alternative, would *choose* to don a skimpy dress, red lipstick and excruciatingly high heels?

Men don't *notice* things about people and are about as articulate as a dumper truck. Never ask a man to report back on what a bride was wearing at a wedding; the only answer you will get is, 'A dress.'

Why *Men* Are Crap!

Men have a ridiculous amount of pride when with their male counterparts. Even if a man runs full pelt into a lamppost he will shrug it off, even pretending that he enjoyed the experience. However, if he is with a female friend, he will writhe in agony, crying out for sympathy like a wounded animal.

Why *Men* Are Crap!

Grooms always look the same. It is the bride who attracts all the attention.

Why *Men* Are Crap!

A man's life expectancy is 20 per cent shorter than a woman's – it's that same old story: he just can't last the distance.

Why *Men* Are Crap!

Whilst it is pitiful that men have a strong desire to compare genital size with one another, it must be emphasised that size *does* matter. Small penises are crap.

Why *Men* Are Crap!

Watching a man dance is like watching a rabid dog trying to escape from a small cage.

Why *Men* Are Crap!

Men are sensitive creatures. You will find in particular two areas of concern: his ego and his genitalia. Both are susceptible to pain.

Why *Men* Are Crap!

Men are five times more likely to kill themselves than women. Pathetic.

Why *Men* Are Crap!

Men are incapable of childbirth. Even if they were the ones having babies, their fear about the prospect of pain would probably mean the end of the human race.

Why *Men* Are Crap!

God made Adam as a practice model. He perfected the human form when he made Eve.

Why *Men* Are Crap!

The Little Man – who spends
his life trying to be Big.

Why *Men* Are Crap!

Why Men are Crap at Sex . . .

Why *Men* Are Crap!

Men hate to use condoms – regardless of the implications that not wearing one will bring. Their definition of safe sex is a padded headboard.

Why *Men* Are Crap!

If a man does bother with foreplay, it is invariably sub-standard. Not many women relish someone blowing in their ear like they are long distance pea-shooting, or twiddling their nipples like they are trying to tune a radio. And it would be nice if the socks came off in time for The Big Moment, too.

Why *Men* Are Crap!

Gentlemen – give the love-bites a miss. A woman does not really want her neck to look as though it has been savaged by next door's Doberman.

Black Widow spiders have the right idea. They kill their men after mating and so stop the snoring before it starts.

The male performance: the reason Viagra was invented. And while on the subject of a poor act, premature ejaculation: just when you thought it was getting good – it's all over.

Why *Men* Are Crap!

A man reaches his sexual peak in life before he knows what to do with it.

Women have more erogenous zones than men but funnily enough, men can't seem to locate a single one.

Why *Men* Are Crap!

A man's definition of foreplay is taking your knickers off.

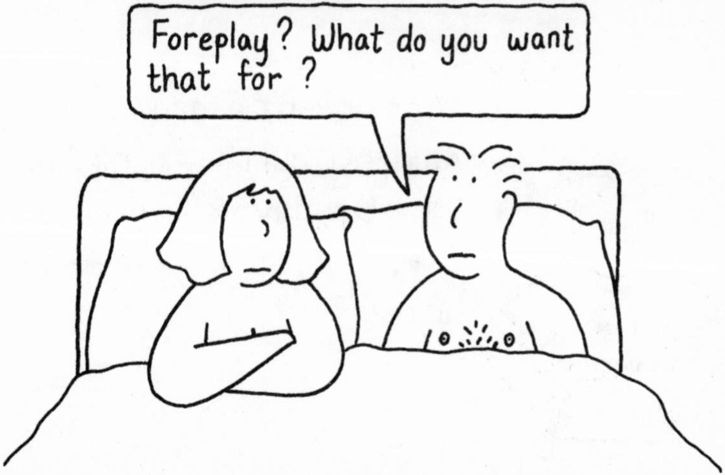
Foreplay? What do you want that for?

Why *Men* Are Crap!

Why doesn't a man understand that kissing him on a Sunday morning is like kissing a pan scourer soaked in beer?

Why *Men* Are Crap!

A man is a discerning creature. He will only chose to have sex with a woman if she breathes.

Why *Men* Are Crap!

Why is it that, just when you think you have met Mr Right, he takes his trousers down to reveal a pair of truly offensive Y-fronts? Game Over.

Why *Men* Are Crap!

One thing you will never hear a woman say:

'What an attractive scrotum you have…'

Why *Men* Are Crap!

Men tend to overheat in bed. Waking up in the middle of the night can be alarming and uncomfortable when you appear to be lying next to a farting, snoring radiator.

Why Men are Stupid . . .

Why *Men* Are Crap!

Electric lawn mowers were invented so that men could find their way back to the house.

Even if a man has everything, he will always need a woman to show him how to work it.

When it comes to men, the word Brain is spelt P-E-N-I-S.

Why *Men* Are Crap!

A man only ever says anything intelligent when he uses as a precursor, 'My wife/girlfriend says ...'

Men are liable to starve
without a tin-opener.

Why *Men* Are Crap!

Only a man would economise on buying a car, in order to install that essential piece of motoring equipment, the stereo, worth at least three times its host's value.

Why *Men* Are Crap!

Men are afraid of cosmetic instruments. This can be beneficial to the female of the species when trying to ward off potential intruders. For extra peace of mind, always keep a pair of eyelash curlers under your pillow.

Why *Men* Are Crap!

The length, potency and audibility of a man's fart are to him and his male friends the measure of his worth. Need we say more?

Why *Men* Are Crap!

A man will wait until the fridge is empty except for half a tin of baked beans and a beer. For two weeks he will survive on take-aways and then think about refilling it – with beer.

Why *Men* Are Crap!

Men do not appear to possess sufficient intelligence to enable them to replace the toilet seat in its rightful, horizontal position.

Why *Men* Are Crap!

Men are only capable of active thought for about five minutes of every hour. Ask him what he is thinking and you'll have to wait for an answer. He needs to pause in order to dream up something constructive to say rather than 'sex', 'food', 'beer', 'sex', 'sport', or 'sex'.

Why *Men* Are Crap!

Diamonds are a woman's best friend, dogs are a man's best friend. I think we can gather which of the sexes is more intelligent.

Why *Men* Are Crap!

When watching a football game (the only thing he can focus on for ten minutes without channel hopping), a man will think that by concentrating really hard, he can actually make a difference to the result. If he shouts loudly at the players/ referee they WILL hear and they WILL do what he says.

Why *Men* Are Crap!

Men do not realise the real value of the phone –

 they see it purely as a means to convey limited, monosyllabic information, therefore failing to discover the potential enjoyment and fulfilment that this instrument can bring.

I ♥ MYSELF

Why *Men* Are Crap!

Why Men are Immature...

Why *Men* Are Crap!

Men have a pathological obsession with keeping the remote control in their possession. This is because:

a) it is a form of gadget

b) without it, a man loses that little bit of control that took him so long to cultivate

c) by nature, he is a selfish creature.

Why *Men* Are Crap!

You do not have to go far to find a man a film he will enjoy. It must simply contain one, or all, of the following components: convent girls, nurses, car chases, gadgets, or lesbians – all of which will drive him to a state of frenzied excitement.

Why *Men* Are Crap!

Why *Men* Are Crap!

Men will not go near the kitchen for ten months of the year, but as soon as the barbecue season comes around, he will monopolise the cooking. 'Barbies' are the ideal opportunity for grand machismo: torching the meat and asserting himself over naked flames.

Why *Men* Are Crap!

A man's handwriting always reflects his personality. It is formulated by the time he is thirteen, and does not change for the rest of his life.

Why *Men* Are Crap!

Due to psychological inferiority complexes, men actually name their penises. They will call their

little friend (the one who does all the thinking) something like 'Rambo' rather than the possibly more appropriate 'Winky'.

Why *Men* Are Crap!

Most men have been given relatively normal names (because their mother had a say). However, amongst themselves they will insist on such flattering and affectionate terms as Shit-face/-head/-for brains.

Men will not, by default, ask for directions. This could explain why Moses was wandering through the wilderness for forty years.

Why *Men* Are Crap!

Why *Men* Are Crap!

Men cannot resist ogling members of the opposite sex. Some men even become builders

and construction workers so they can do this freely. To ensure a positive response some even let their trousers expose most of their buttocks. This is a particularly crap form of male.

Why *Men* Are Crap!

Rather than as a delicious food, curries are regarded by men as a passport to an ensuing 'ring-stinger' – something a man must experience in order to exert his true 'masculinity'.

Why *Men* Are Crap!

It is rare to find a man who is remotely sensitive. The only men who are sensitive, caring and compassionate have boyfriends.

Why *Men* Are Crap!

If you want to dump your man, tell him you love him. If this *doesn't* work, ask him to marry you. If this doesn't work, tell him you want to have his babies. Now blink, and you will *not* see him for dust.

Why *Men* Are Crap!

Girls grow out of toys by the time they reach their teens – men carry on needing 'gadgets' to play with for the rest of their lives. If it is shiny, has buttons and follows commands, it not only provides endless entertainment but also gives a man status with his friends.

Why *Men* Are Crap!

James Bond was created to give men a false sense of identity and something to aspire to. This is why they have no qualms about actually thinking they *are* Bond when in the car or playing with a gadget such as a personal organiser or, even more tragically, the remote control.

Why *Men* Are Crap!

When it comes to rituals, there is one that men have a strange predilection for – that of taking down the trousers and sticking out the posterior to expose white, hairy buttocks. This ritual provides particular enjoyment when performed in public.

Why *Men* Are Crap!

Women gain confidence through achievement. Men rarely experience achievement, so gain theirs through a deluded association with their superheroes, often remembered from childhood. Many Clark Kents think they are actually Supermen.

Why *Men* Are Crap!

They will never admit it, but men sulk like babies.

The male sulk involves extended periods of pouting and silence, as well as the slamming shut, or down, of anything they can get their hands on. It is dangerous to say anything to a man in a sulk.

Why *Men* Are Crap!

BEWARE
MAN
SULKING

Why *Men* Are Crap!

The words 'commitment' and 'monogamy' are as

repugnant to a man as having his head flushed down a toilet. If, by a strange turn of events, you wish to attract a man and be with him for any amount of time, never use these words in any form of conversation.

Why *Men* Are Crap!

Women can pay each other compliments; if a man pays another man a compliment his heterosexual friends will KNOW that (without doubt) he is gay.

Why *Men* Are Crap!

Men take longer to mature. In fact, most men don't seem to get past adolescence. It is appropriate, therefore, to talk to them as you would a naughty child.

Why Men are Gross . . .

Why *Men* Are Crap!

Men's magazines often feature pictures of naked women. Women's magazines also feature pictures of naked women. This is because the female body is beautiful and sleek, whereas the male body is lumpy and hairy.

Why *Men* Are Crap!

Men with breasts. These creatures are not only offensive, they are entirely brazen in flaunting their mammaries. They should learn to:

a) *be* ashamed
b) *not* wear tight T-shirts
c) *never* remove said T-shirt in public.

Why *Men* Are Crap!

Never be lulled into thinking that a man is above the attractions of a soft porn magazine. He

may act nonchalant when you are around, but when with friends he will pore over the magazine, salivating with excitement – which is nothing compared to how he looks at it when on his own . . .

Why *Men* Are Crap!

Why *Men* Are Crap!

It's Saturday morning and you run a hot bubble bath. The bathroom seemed perfectly normal when you left it; now there is a malodorous smell permeating the atmosphere. The culprit can be found lying in bed and smiling smugly, as he reads the sports section of his favourite paper.

Why *Men* Are Crap!

Although acceptable in small children and dogs, a man shovelling food into his mouth at a rate of knots, chewing with slack jaw and dribbling is not considered good restaurant etiquette.

Why *Men* Are Crap!

Women realise that urinating, for a man, is VERY CLEVER. But how difficult can it be to direct the urine INTO the toilet?

Why *Men* Are Crap!

The male of the species displays a tendency to stare vacantly into the middle distance while readjusting/scratching his scrotal region – a charming habit, which it is a pleasure to be exposed to.

Why *Men* Are Crap!

Men only realise their pants and socks need to be washed when a strange fungal substance forms on the insides.

Why Men are Dull . . .

Why *Men* Are Crap!

Men are unable to enjoy the art form that is gossiping. You can try to get them interested but (unless you are telling him about your two female best friends making love to each other) his attention span will last for approximately twenty seconds.

Why *Men* Are Crap!

Whilst a woman's Saturday night (if she is staying in) may involve a good book, good food and a deep bath, a man's Saturday night is always dictated by a football game or, more tragically, mind-numbing lists of football results.

Why *Men* Are Crap!

Men have a fanatical desire to arrange their possessions in alphabetical order; and the

saddest cases have also been known to catalogue said possessions. Take particular heed when you see a man using his personal organiser to do this.

Why *Men* Are Crap!

Golf. Men who don't play this game differ little from those who do. They are still obsessed with the length of their club, the distance of their shot, and whether they can get a hole in one.

Why Men are Pigs . . .

Why *Men* Are Crap!

A man will plead grave illness and go to bed at the first sign of a headache. However, he is never too ill to fantasize that Nursey-Nursey will come and look after him.

Why *Men* Are Crap!

Why *Men* Are Crap!

One of the most abhorrent forms of male is he who talks to a woman with his eyes permanently fixed on her breasts. When will men learn that this particular region, when talked at, is not receptive?

Why *Men* Are Crap!

Men lie 99 per cent of the time. The only time they tell the truth is when it is the most tactless thing to do. The classic example being, 'Yes, your bum *does* look big in that'.

Why *Men* Are Crap!

Why *Men* Are Crap!

Men buy a newspaper purely to get excited/
depressed about the latest
sports result/property prices/
car prices – and you are treated
to a loud running commentary.
Your response must be highly
animated, or you may be
exposed to one of his sulks.

I ♥ MYSELF

Why *Men* Are Crap!

A mild pheromonal smell can be attractive, but five days' stale sweat? Unacceptable behaviour – such an animal should be put behind bars.

Why *Men* Are Crap!

Men think that picking their feet up when you are vacuuming is 'helping with the housework'.

Why *Men* Are Crap!

Men are incapable of having 'a few drinks'. One will invariably turn into two, then three, then twenty. Then they will do one (or all) of the following:

a) Spew vomit over the bar/someone's feet/the table

b) Pass out cold in a flower bed

c) Phone every woman they know, saying they love them.

Why *Men* Are Crap!

Why *Men* Are Crap!

The ultimate reason why men are crap?

Because they're not women!

Why *Men* Are Crap!

10 Things You Will Never Hear a Man Say . . .

Why *Men* Are Crap!

1) Can I get you anything while I'm up?

2) I've been wrong all along,
and you are so right.

Why *Men* Are Crap!

3) I don't blame you for not being able to find it on the map, these roads are so confusing. I think we need to stop and ask for directions.

4) Let's go shopping. You can try on clothes while I hold your handbag.

5) Actually, I think her breasts are just too big.

6) Personally, I wouldn't like to bed [insert nubile film starlet]. I think she lacks personality.

Why *Men* Are Crap!

7) Have you had a haircut? It looks fantastic!

8) I don't believe in one night stands.

9) I'm not fussy. I just want a car that gets me from A to B. That's all they are made for, after all.

Why *Men* Are Crap!

10) I wouldn't be able even to contemplate the idea of you and your best friend in bed together.

**For the latest humour books
from Summersdale, check out**

www.summersdale.com